HIGH SCHOOL MUS

for alto sax

ISBN-13: 978-1-4234-5406-9
ISBN-10: 1-4234-5406-5

Walt Disney Music Company
Wonderland Music Company, Inc.

DISTRIBUTED BY

HAL•LEONARD®
CORPORATION

7777 W. Bluemound Rd. P.O. Box 13819 Milwaukee, WI 53213

Visit Hal Leonard Online at
www.halleonard.com

CONTENTS

BOP TO THE TOP

ALTO SAX

Words and Music by RANDY PETERSEN
and KEVIN QUINN

Latin Dance groove

f
To Coda
ff
mf
D.S. al Coda
f
CODA
ff

BREAKING FREE

ALTO SAX

Words and Music by
JAMIE HOUSTON

f
mf
f
mp legato
rit.

GET'CHA HEAD IN THE GAME

ALTO SAX

Words and Music by RAY CHAM,
GREG CHAM and ANDREW SEELEY

f
Play 3 times
To Coda
mp legato
D.S. al Coda
(with repeats)
f
CODA
(Spoken:) Get - 'cha, get - 'cha, get - 'cha, get - 'cha head in the game. Whoo!

I CAN'T TAKE MY EYES OFF OF YOU

ALTO SAX

Words and Music by MATTHEW GERRARD
and ROBBIE NEVIL

mf
f
1.
f
2.
ff

START OF SOMETHING NEW

ALTO SAX

Words and Music by MATTHEW GERRARD
and ROBBIE NEVIL

D.S. al Coda
CODA
mf
f
1.
mf
2.
decresc.
rit.
mp

STICK TO THE STATUS QUO

ALTO SAX

Words and Music by DAVID N. LAWRENCE
and FAYE GREENBERG

Moderately fast

cresc.
f
p cresc.
ff
mf
f
1.
2.

WE'RE ALL IN THIS TOGETHER

ALTO SAX

Words and Music by MATTHEW GERRARD
and ROBBIE NEVIL

mf
1.
2.
D.S. al Coda
CODA
f
1.
2.
ff

WHAT I'VE BEEN LOOKING FOR

ALTO SAX

Words and Music by ANDY DODD and ADAM WATTS

To Coda
mf
D.S. al Coda
f
CODA

WHEN THERE WAS ME AND YOU

ALTO SAX

Words and Music by
JAMIE HOUSTON

mp
f
f
mf
rit.
mp

HAL•LEONARD
INSTRUMENTAL
PLAY-ALONG

WITH THESE FANTASTIC BOOK/CD PACKS, INSTRUMENTALISTS CAN PLAY ALONG WITH THEIR FAVORITE SONGS!

BROADWAY'S BEST

15 Broadway favorites arranged for the instrumentalist, including: Always Look on the Bright Side of Life • Any Dream Will Do • Castle on a Cloud • I Whistle a Happy Tune • My Favorite Things • Where Is Love? • and more.

- 00841974 Flute $10.95
- 00841975 Clarinet $10.95
- 00841976 Alto Sax.................$10.95
- 00841977 Tenor Sax..............$10.95
- 00841978 Trumpet................$10.95
- 00841979 Horn.....................$10.95
- 00841980 Trombone..............$10.95
- 00841981 Violin....................$10.95
- 00841982 Viola.....................$10.95
- 00841983 Cello.....................$10.95

CHRISTMAS CAROLS

15 favorites from the holidays, including: Deck the Hall • The First Noel • Good King Wenceslas • Hark! the Herald Angels Sing • It Came upon the Midnight Clear • O Christmas Tree • We Three Kings of Orient Are • and more.

- 00842132 Flute $10.95
- 00842133 Clarinet $10.95
- 00842134 Alto Sax.................$10.95
- 00842135 Tenor Sax..............$10.95
- 00842136 Trumpet................$10.95
- 00842137 Horn.....................$10.95
- 00842138 Trombone..............$10.95
- 00842139 Violin....................$10.95
- 00842140 Viola.....................$10.95
- 00842141 Cello.....................$10.95

CHRISTMAS FAVORITES

Includes 15 holiday favorites with a play-along CD: Blue Christmas • Caroling, Caroling • The Christmas Song (Chestnuts Roasting on an Open Fire) • Christmas Time Is Here • Do You Hear What I Hear • Here Comes Santa Claus (Right Down Santa Claus Lane) • (There's No Place Like) Home for the Holidays • I Saw Mommy Kissing Santa Claus • Little Saint Nick • Merry Christmas, Darling • O Bambino • Rudolph the Red-Nosed Reindeer • Santa Claus Is Comin' to Town • Snowfall

- 00841964 Flute $10.95
- 00841965 Clarinet $10.95
- 00841966 Alto Sax.................$10.95
- 00841967 Tenor Sax..............$10.95
- 00841968 Trumpet................$10.95
- 00841969 Horn.....................$10.95
- 00841970 Trombone..............$10.95
- 00841971 Violin....................$10.95
- 00841972 Viola.....................$10.95
- 00841973 Cello.....................$10.95

CLASSICAL FAVORITES

15 classic solos for all instrumentalists. Includes: Ave Maria (Schubert) • Blue Danube Waltz (Strauss, Jr.) • Für Elise (Beethoven) • Largo (Handel) • Minuet in G (Bach) • Ode to Joy (Beethoven) • Symphony No. 9 in E Minor ("From the New World"), Second Movement Excerpt (Dvorak) • and more.

- 00841954 Flute $10.95
- 00841955 Clarinet $10.95
- 00841956 Alto Sax.................$10.95
- 00841957 Tenor Sax..............$10.95
- 00841958 Trumpet................$10.95
- 00841959 Horn.....................$10.95
- 00841960 Trombone..............$10.95
- 00841961 Violin....................$10.95
- 00841962 Viola.....................$10.95
- 00841963 Cello.....................$10.95

CONTEMPORARY HITS

Play 15 of your pop favorites along with this great folio and full accompaniment CD. Songs include: Accidentally in Love • Calling All Angels • Don't Tell Me • Everything • Fallen • The First Cut Is the Deepest • Here Without You • Hey Ya! • If I Ain't Got You • It's My Life • 100 Years • Take My Breath Away (Love Theme) • This Love • White Flag • You Raise Me Up.

- 00841924 Flute $12.95
- 00841925 Clarinet $12.95
- 00841926 Alto Sax.................$12.95
- 00841927 Tenor Sax..............$10.95
- 00841928 Trumpet................$10.95
- 00841929 Horn.....................$10.95
- 00841930 Trombone..............$10.95
- 00841931 Violin....................$12.95
- 00841932 Viola.....................$12.95
- 00841933 Cello.....................$10.95

DISNEY GREATS

Another great play-along collection of 15 Disney favorites, including: Arabian Nights • A Change in Me • Hawaiian Roller Coaster Ride • I'm Still Here (Jim's Theme) • It's a Small World • Look Through My Eyes • Supercalifragilisticexpialidocious • Where the Dream Takes You • Yo Ho (A Pirate's Life for Me) • and more.

- 00841934 Flute $12.95
- 00842078 Oboe.....................$12.95
- 00841935 Clarinet $12.95
- 00841936 Alto Sax.................$12.95
- 00841937 Tenor Sax..............$12.95
- 00841938 Trumpet................$12.95
- 00841939 Horn.....................$12.95
- 00841940 Trombone..............$12.95
- 00841941 Violin....................$12.95
- 00841942 Viola.....................$12.95
- 00841943 Cello.....................$12.95

ESSENTIAL ROCK

Instrumentalists will love jamming with a play-along CD for 15 top rock classics, including: Aqualung • Brown Eyed Girl • Crocodile Rock • Don't Stop • Free Bird • I Want You to Want Me • La Grange • Low Rider • Maggie May • Walk This Way • and more.

- 00841944 Flute $10.95
- 00841945 Clarinet $10.95
- 00841946 Alto Sax.................$10.95
- 00841947 Tenor Sax..............$10.95
- 00841948 Trumpet................$10.95
- 00841949 Horn.....................$10.95
- 00841950 Trombone..............$10.95
- 00841951 Violin....................$10.95
- 00841952 Viola.....................$10.95
- 00841953 Cello.....................$10.95

HIGH SCHOOL MUSICAL

Solo arrangements with CD accompaniment for 9 hits from the wildly popular Disney Channel original movie. Songs include: Bop to the Top • Breaking Free • Get'cha Head in the Game • I Can't Take My Eyes Off of You • Start of Something New • Stick to the Status Quo • We're All in This Together • What I've Been Looking For • When There Was Me and You.

- 00842121 Flute $10.95
- 00842122 Clarinet $10.95
- 00842123 Alto Sax.................$10.95
- 00842124 Tenor Sax..............$10.95
- 00842125 Trumpet................$10.95
- 00842126 Horn.....................$10.95
- 00842127 Trombone..............$10.95
- 00842128 Violin....................$10.95
- 00842129 Viola.....................$10.95
- 00842130 Cello.....................$10.95

ANDREW LLOYD WEBBER CLASSICS

12 solos from Webber's greatest shows complete with full band accompaniment on CD. Titles include: As If We Never Said Goodbye • Close Every Door • Don't Cry for Me Argentina • Everything's Alright • Go Go Go Joseph • Gus: The Theatre Cat • Love Changes Everything • The Music of the Night • Our Kind of Love • The Phantom of the Opera • Unexpected Song • Whistle Down the Wind.

- 00841824 Flute $14.95
- 00841825 Oboe.....................$14.95
- 00841826 Clarinet $14.95
- 00841827 Alto Sax.................$14.95
- 00841828 Tenor Sax..............$14.95
- 00841829 Trumpet................$14.95
- 00841830 Horn.....................$14.95
- 00841831 Trombone..............$14.95
- 00841832 Mallet Percussion ..$14.95
- 00841833 Violin....................$14.95
- 00841834 Viola.....................$14.95
- 00841835 Cello.....................$14.95

MOVIE MUSIC

15 hits from popular movie blockbusters of today, including: And All That Jazz • Come What May • I Am a Man of Constant Sorrow • I Believe I Can Fly • I Walk the Line • Seasons of Love • Theme from Spider Man • and more

- 00842089 Flute $10.95
- 00842090 Clarinet $10.95
- 00842091 Alto Sax.................$10.95
- 00842092 Tenor Sax..............$10.95
- 00842093 Trumpet................$10.95
- 00842094 Horn.....................$10.95
- 00842095 Trombone..............$10.95
- 00842096 Violin....................$10.95
- 00842097 Viola.....................$10.95
- 00842098 Cello.....................$10.95

TV FAVORITES

15 TV tunes arranged for instrumentalists, including: The Addams Family Theme • The Brady Bunch • Green Acres Theme • Happy Days • Johnny's Theme • Linus and Lucy • NFL on Fox Theme • Theme from The Simpsons • and more.

- 00842079 Flute $10.95
- 00842080 Clarinet $10.95
- 00842081 Alto Sax.................$10.95
- 00842082 Tenor Sax..............$10.95
- 00842083 Trumpet................$10.95
- 00842084 Horn.....................$10.95
- 00842085 Trombone..............$10.95
- 00842086 Violin....................$10.95
- 00842087 Viola.....................$10.95
- 00842088 Cello.....................$10.95

For More Information, See Your Local Music Dealer, Or Write To:

HAL•LEONARD® CORPORATION
7777 W. Bluemound Rd. P.O. Box 13819 Milwaukee, WI 53213

Prices, contents and availability are subject to change without notice.

Some products may not be available outside the U.S.A.

Visit Hal Leonard online at
WWW.HALLEONARD.COM